# Read All About

# CATS

by Jaclyn Jaycox

raintree

a Capstone company — publishers for children

Raintree is an imprint of Capstone Global Library Limited, a company incorporated in England and Wales having its registered office at 264 Banbury Road, Oxford, OX2 7DY – Registered company number: 6695582

www.raintree.co.uk
myorders@raintree.co.uk

Text © Capstone Global Library Limited 2021
The moral rights of the proprietor have been asserted.

Designed by Kayla Rossow
Original illustrations © Capstone Global Library Limited 2021
Picture research by Morgan Walters
Production by Katy LaVigne
Originated by Capstone Global Library Ltd
Printed and bound in India

978 1 3982 0318 1 (hardback)
978 1 3982 0317 4 (paperback)

British Library Cataloguing in Publication Data
A full catalogue record for this book is available from the British Library.

Acknowledgements
We would like to thank the following for permission to reproduce photographs: Shutterstock: 4clover, (watercolour) Cover, design element throughout, 5 second Studio, top right 14, Africa Studio, middle right 29, Alexey Kozhemyakin, bottom right 14, Alina Simakova, 16, Ambiento, middle left 9, Andrew Ivan, bottom left 10, Andrey Stratilatov, top 27, Angela Kotsell, top left 26, ANURAK PONGPATIMET, 12, top left 29, Bartkowski, bottom left 13, bmf-foto.de, 24, Chendongshan, top 15, top 25, Chris Mirek Freeman, bottom 31, DenisNata, middle left 21, didesign021, bottom 30, Edwin Butter, top right 6, Elya Vatel, bottom 15, Eric Isselee, top right 10, top left 17, Erik Lam, 4, Ermolaev Alexander, middle left 18, bottom right 18, fantom_rd, top right 23, Fesus Robert, middle left 14, Impact Photography, top 31, Jemastock, design element, Kasefoto, 8, top left 11, Kelvin Degree, design element, Kolomenskaya Kseniya, bottom right 9, Konjushenko Vladimir, bottom left 17, Konstanttin, top right 26, Krissi Lundgren, middle right 11, Kuttelvaserova Stuchelova, bottom right 21, Lainea, bottom left 11, MaxyM, bottom 27, Michael Potter11, middle left 5, Milles Studio, top 30, Natalia Belotelova, top right 9, Nejron Photo, bottom left 6, New Africa, bottom right 7, Nils Jacobi, bottom Cover, top right 21, Nneirda, top 22, Oleksandr Lytvynenko, middle right 17, 28, Ondrej Chvatal, bottom right 5, Osaze Cuomo, middle left 23, panuwat phimpha, bottom 25, Panyawatt, top right Cover, Pavel Shlykov, bottom right 19, Peter Wollinga, 1, PHOTOCREO Michal Bednarek, bottom right 23, Playa del Carmen, bottom left 29, Popova Valeriya, bottom left 5, Rashid Valitov, top left 13, ReVelStockArt, design element, rukxstockphoto, middle right 13, s_derevianko, 20, schankz, bottom 22, Scorpp, middle 13, Sergey Zaykov, top 7, Shawna and Damien Richard, middle right 18, Sonsedska Yuliia, top left 18, Svineyard, bottom 26, Tsekhmister, bottom right 13, turlakova, top right 19, Ukki Studio, top left 19, Volonoff, design element throughout.

Every effort has been made to contact copyright holders of material reproduced in this book. Any omissions will be rectified in subsequent printings if notice is given to the publisher.

All the internet addresses (URLs) given in this book were valid at the time of going to press. However, due to the dynamic nature of the internet, some addresses may have changed, or sites may have changed or ceased to exist since publication. While the author and publisher regret any inconvenience this may cause readers, no responsibility for any such changes can be accepted by either the author or the publisher.

# Contents

Chapter 1
## History of cats . . . . . . . . . . 4

Chapter 2
## Cat breeds . . . . . . . . . . 8

Chapter 3
## Life cycle . . . . . . . . . . . 12

Chapter 4
## Cat bodies . . . . . . . . . . . 16

Chapter 5
## Senses . . . . . . . . . . . . . 20

Chapter 6
## Cat behaviour . . . . . . . . . 24

Chapter 7
## Caring for your pet . . . . . . 28

Glossary . . . . . . . . . . . . . . . . . . . 32
Index . . . . . . . . . . . . . . . . . . . . . 32

Words in **bold** are in the glossary.

# Chapter 1

# History of cats

Cats have been around for thousands of years. People used to think they were **sacred**. Let's find out more about the history of these furry **felines**.

There are more than 600 million cats in the world.

Scientists believe cats came from North African wildcats.

All cats belong to the same **species**, called Felis catus.

lion

Lions, tigers and leopards are related to cats.

leopard

tiger

Cats are mammals. Mammals breathe air. They give birth to live young.

Cats were first drawn to humans living on farms. There were lots of mice around to catch!

In ancient Egypt, people dressed cats in jewels.

The United States Post Office hired cats in the late 1800s to keep mice away.

Cat litter was invented in 1947. Kittens and indoor cats use litter trays.

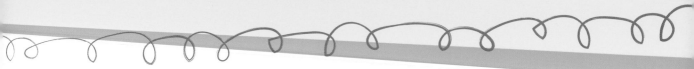

# Chapter 2

# Cat breeds

There are many **breeds** of cats. Breeds have different sizes and colours. Each breed has special features.

The International Cat Association recognizes 71 different cat breeds.

There are six breeds of hairless cats.

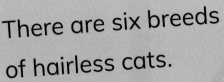

Designer cats come from two different **purebred** parents. Each parent is a different breed.

Savannah is a type of designer breed. Some cost as much as £23,000 to buy!

Maine coons are one of the most popular cat breeds.

American shorthairs are one of the best breeds for hunting mice.

The Abyssinian is one of the oldest cat breeds.

The Singapura is the smallest breed. Some weigh only 2 kilograms (4 pounds)!

British shorthair cats have blue fur.

# Chapter 3

# Life cycle

Cats go through different stages of life. Playful kittens become loving cats. Let's see how they grow and change.

Cats go through six stages of life: kitten, junior, prime, mature, senior and geriatric.

Females give birth to an average of three to five kittens in each litter.

Kittens don't open their eyes until they are one to two weeks old.

All kittens are born with blue eyes. Only a few breeds have blue eyes as adults.

The first six months of a cat's life is equivalent to 10 human years!

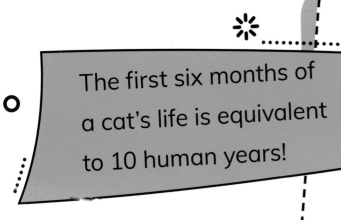

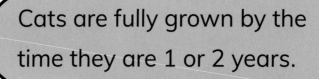

Cats are fully grown by the time they are 1 or 2 years.

On average, cats live for about 15 years.

Cats are adults when they reach the prime stage.

Cats are most playful during the kitten stage.

The oldest ever cat lived to be 38 years old.

# Chapter 4

# Cat bodies

Each cat looks different. But their bodies are mostly the same. They are perfectly designed to be great hunters.

Compared to their body size, cats have the biggest eyes of any mammal.

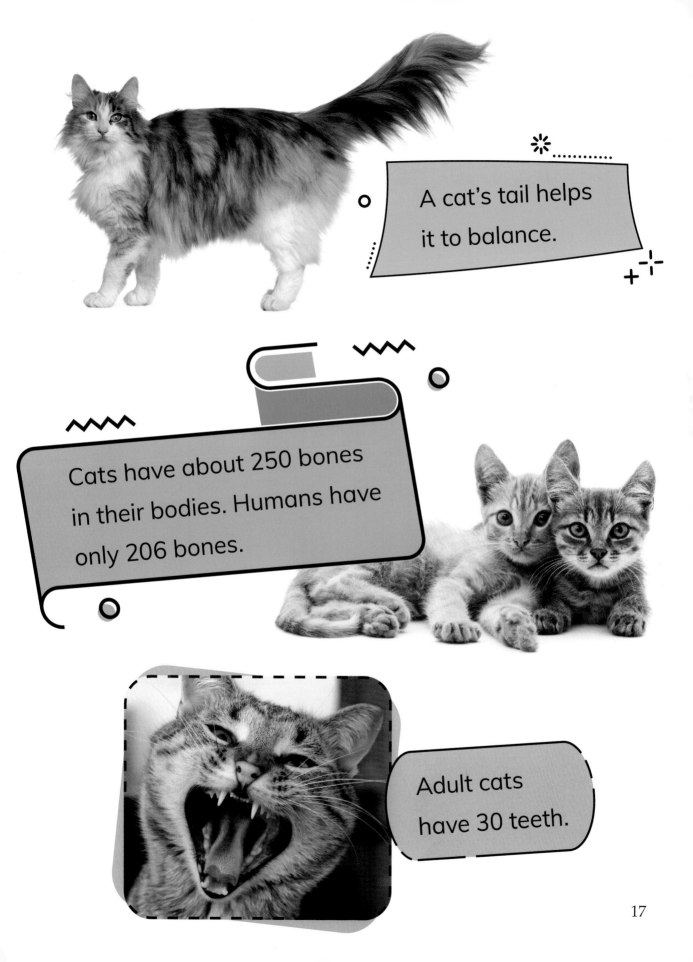

A cat's tail helps it to balance.

Cats have about 250 bones in their bodies. Humans have only 206 bones.

Adult cats have 30 teeth.

Cats have five toes on each of their front paws. Each back paw has four toes.

Only female cats can have three or more colours in their fur.

A cat's tongue has little hooks on it. The hooks brush the cat's fur when it licks itself.

Cats sweat only through their paws.

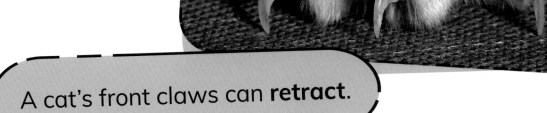

A cat's front claws can **retract**.

# Chapter 5

# Senses

Cats' **senses** help them to explore the world.
Some cat senses are stronger than a human's.
They help cats to survive in the wild.

Cats are colour blind. Some people believe cats can see only blue and grey.

Cats can see in darkness six times better than humans.

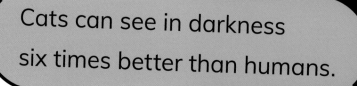

Cats hear much better than humans and even dogs.

Every cat has a different nose print.

A cat's sense of smell is 14 times better than a human's.

Cats don't have a strong sense of taste. They can't taste sweet foods at all.

A cat's whiskers are very sensitive. They can feel very small temperature changes.

Cats are nearsighted. It's hard for them to see objects that are far away.

Cats have a blind spot. They can't see things right under their noses.

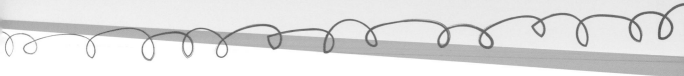

# Chapter 6

# Cat behaviour

Have you ever wondered what a cat is thinking? Watching a cat's behaviour could give you the answer. Find out what their sounds and actions mean.

Cats rub against things to leave their scent. The scent tells other animals that's their **territory**.

Cats can make around 100 sounds. Dogs only make about 10 sounds.

Cats don't miaow at other cats. They only miaow at humans.

A cat's purr can mean it's happy. But cats also purr to calm themselves if they are stressed.

Cats can make different facial expressions.

Cats copy the sounds that birds make.

If a cat wraps its tail around you, the cat is giving you a hug!

Cats sometimes bring caught mice to their owners. Maybe they think it's a nice present!

Cats sleep an average of 15 hours a day!

# Chapter 7

# Caring for your pet

Cats make wonderful pets. There is a lot to know about taking care of them. It's important to keep them safe, happy and healthy!

Cats and dogs can get live together in the same household.

Some cats like cuddles, but not all of them. Get to know your own cat's likes and dislikes.

Cats need fresh water and food every day. A small number of treats is OK too!

Indoor cats should have their litter trays cleaned every day.

Cats should see a vet at least once a year.

Cats' teeth should be kept clean.

Cats should have **vaccinations** to keep them healthy.

Cats usually keep themselves clean. But make sure you brush their fur!

A cat should wear a collar with an ID tag and bell when going outside.

## Glossary

**breed** group of animals that look and act alike

**feline** of the cat family

**purebred** having parents of the same breed

**retract** slide in or out

**sacred** very special

**sense** way of knowing about your surroundings; hearing, smell, touch, taste and sight are the five senses

**species** group of animals with similar features

**territory** area of land that an animal roams in

**vaccination** medicine given to help prevent a certain illness

## Index

age 13–15

birth 6, 13

colour 8, 11, 18, 20

ears 21
eyes 13, 16, 20–21, 23

fur 9, 11, 18, 31

hunting 6–7, 10, 16, 27

mammals 6, 16

paws 18–19

playing 12, 15

relatives 4–5

size 8, 11, 14, 16
sounds 24–26
species 5

tails 17, 26
teeth 17, 30

vets 30